Our School

Healthy Living

We walk to school.

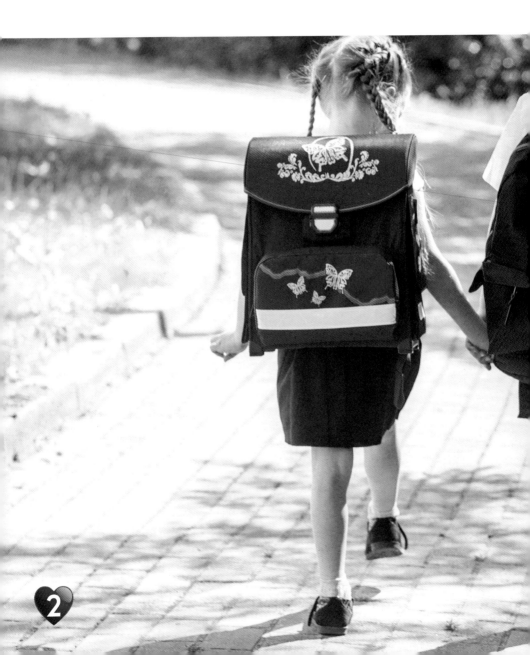

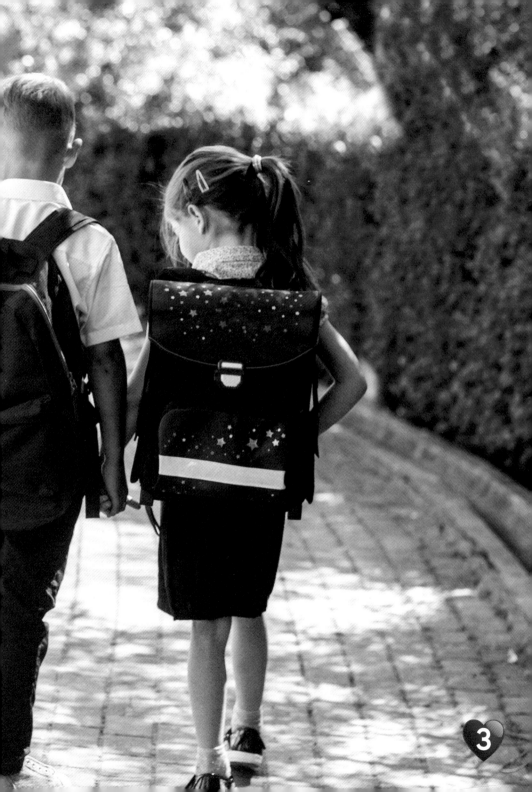

Here is our school.

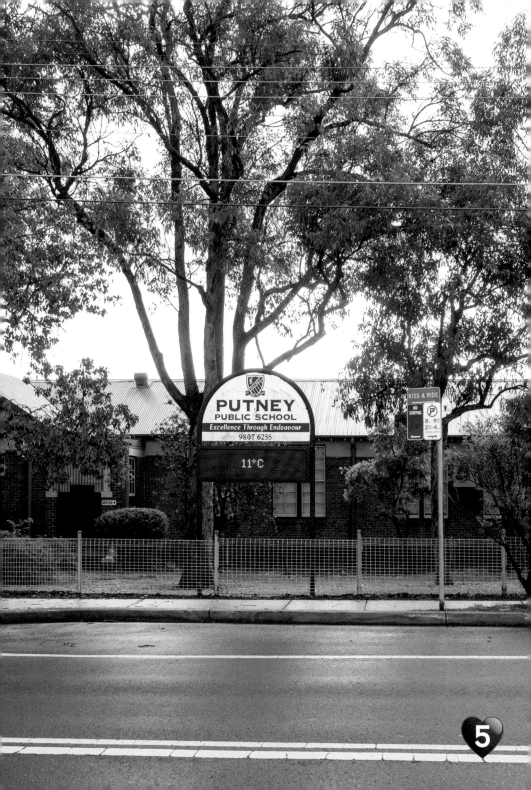

Here are our bags.

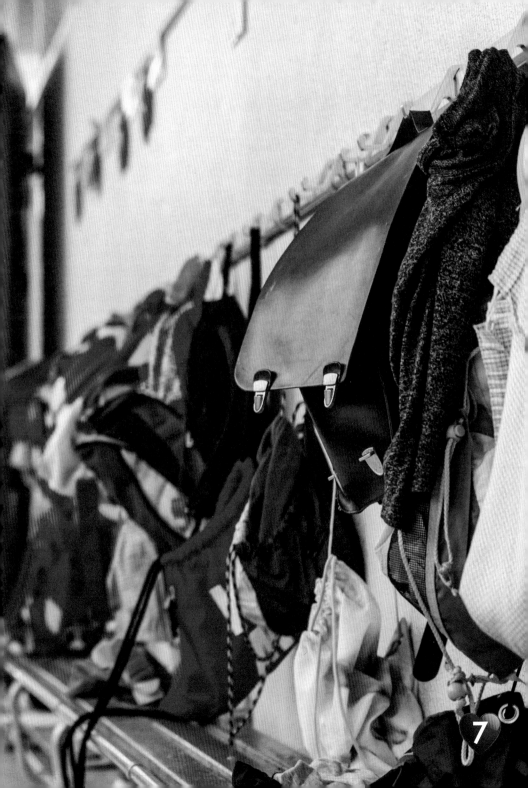

Here are our seats.

8

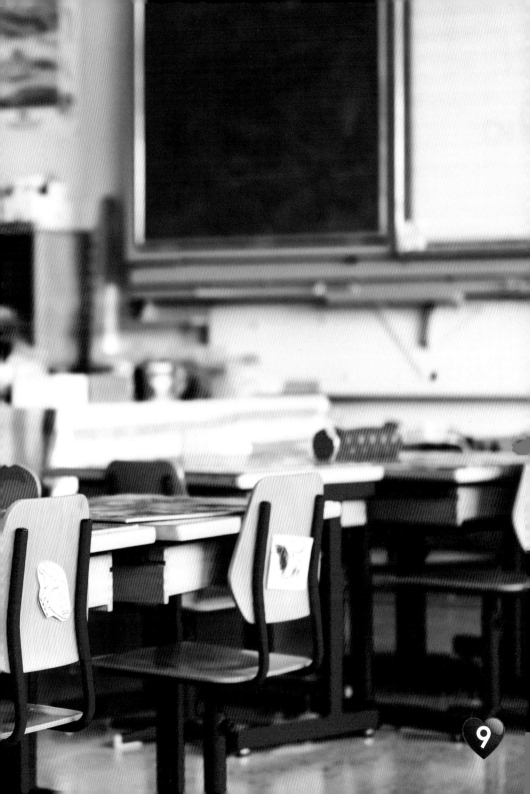

We read
in the library.

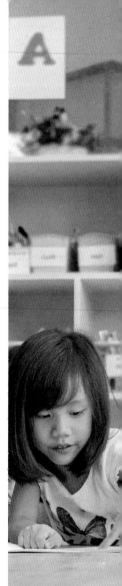

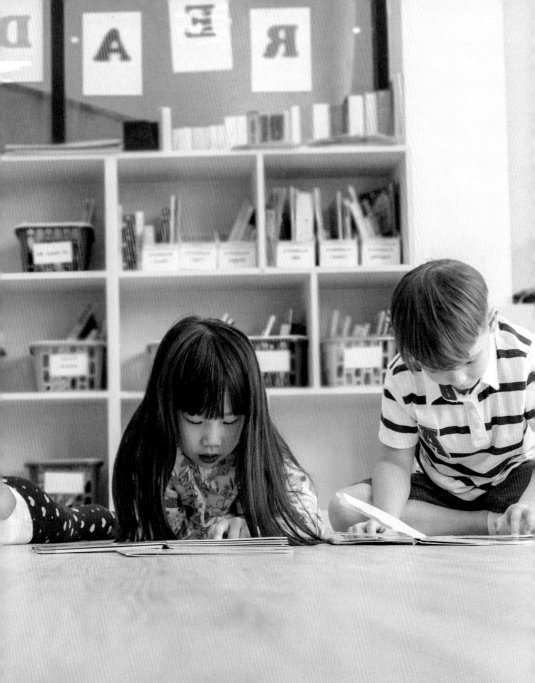

We climb

in the gym.

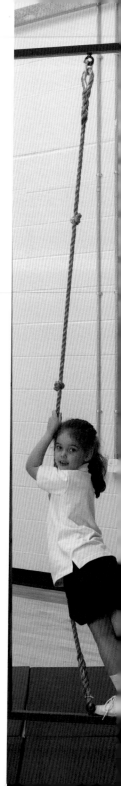

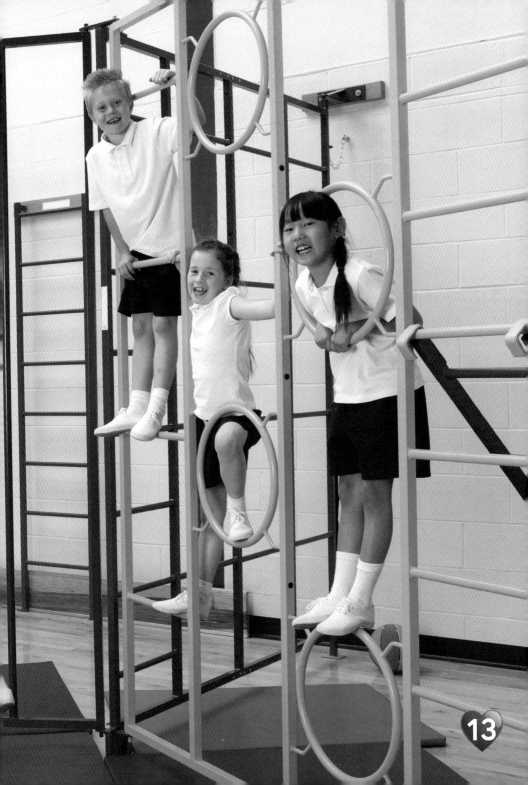

13

We line up

in the playground.

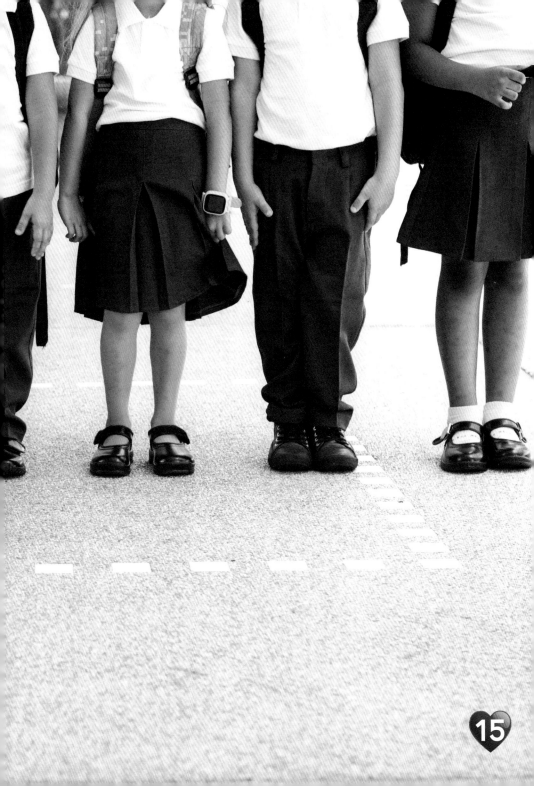

15

We love our school.

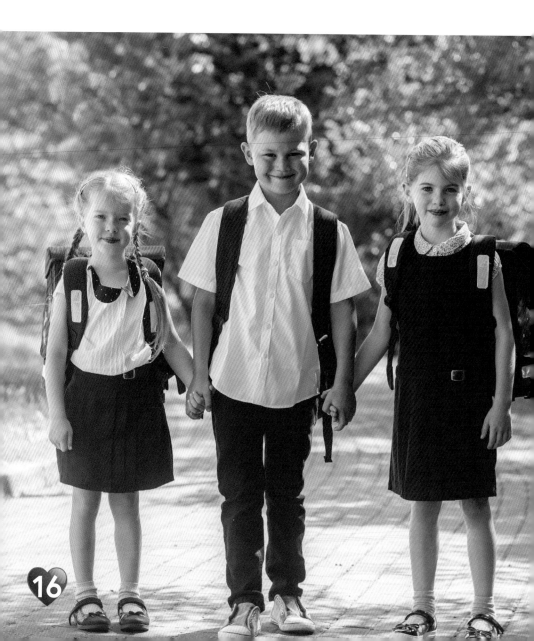